TRIBES of NATIVE AMERICA

Chinook

edited by Marla Felkins Ryan
and Linda Schmittroth

BLACKBIRCH®
PRESS

San Diego • Detroit • New York • San Francisco • Cleveland
New Haven, Conn. • Waterville, Maine • London • Munich

THOMSON

✳

GALE

Photo credits: Cover Courtesy of Northwestern University Library; cover © National Archives; cover © Photospin; cover © Perry Jasper Photography; cover © Picturequest; cover © Seattle Post-Intelligencer Collection, Museum of History & Industry; cover © PhotoDisc; cover, pages 12, 22 © Library of Congress; page 5 © Corel; page 6 © Dave G. houser/Corbis; pages 7, 9, 25 © North Wind Picture Archives; pages 8, 27 © Hulton|Archive by Getty Images; page 10 © MSCUA, University of Washington Libraries, NA4034; page 13 © Corbis; page 14 © Gary Braasch/Corbis; pages 17, 30 © AP Photo/Mark Duncan; pages 18, 19, 20, 21(bottom), 23 (top), 26, 28 © Marilyn "Angel" Wynn/Nativestock.com; page 21(top) © Brandon D. Cole/Corbis; page 24 © Mary Evans Picture Library; page 29 © MSCUA, University of washington Libraries, NA3888; page 31 © Connie Ricca/Corbis

LIBRARY OF CONGRESS CATALOGING-IN-PUBLICATION DATA

Chinook / Marla Felkins Ryan, book editor ; Linda Schmittroth, book editor.
   v. cm. — (Tribes of Native America)
Includes bibliographical references and index.
Contents: Name — History — Government — Daily life — Current tribal issues.
  ISBN 1-56711-685-X (alk. paper)
  1. Chinook Indians—History—Juvenile literature. 2. Chinook Indians—Social life and customs—Juvenile literature. [1. Chinook Indians. 2. Indians of North America—Northwest, Pacific.] I. Ryan, Marla Felkins. II. Schmittroth, Linda. III. Series.

  E99.C57C45 2003
  979.5004'9741—dc21

                                                2003002627

Printed in United States
10 9 8 7 6 5 4 3 2 1

Table of Contents

• FIRST LOOK •

CHINOOK

Name

Chinook (pronounced *shi-NOOK*).

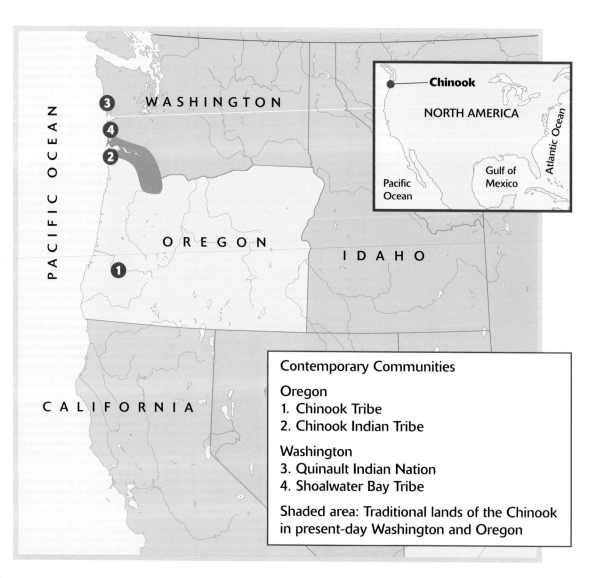

Contemporary Communities

Oregon
1. Chinook Tribe
2. Chinook Indian Tribe

Washington
3. Quinault Indian Nation
4. Shoalwater Bay Tribe

Shaded area: Traditional lands of the Chinook in present-day Washington and Oregon

Where are the traditional Chinook lands?

The Chinook first lived in parts of present-day Washington and Oregon. Their home was along the shore of the Columbia River. Today, the Chinook are broken up into three groups. The Shoalwater Bay Chinook live on the Shoalwater Reservation in Pacific County, Washington. The Wahkiakum Chinook live on the Quinault Reservation in the southwest corner of Washington's Olympic Peninsula. The Chinook Indian Tribe lives in several towns and cities in Oregon and Washington.

The Chinook have lived along the Columbia River (pictured), in areas of what are now Oregon and Washington State, for thousands of years.

What has happened to the population?

In 1825 there were about 720 Chinook. In 1840 there were only 280. In a 1990 population count by the U.S. Bureau of the Census, 813 people said they were Chinook. Of this group, 32 said they were Clatsop and 33 said they were members of other Chinook groups.

Origins and group ties

The Chinook have lived in their homeland for thousands of years. The Chinook Nation was made up of many tribes. The nation included the Cathlapotle, the Kathlamet, the Clatsop, the Clackamas, the Multnomah, and the formal Chinook Tribe. This tribe was also called the Lower Chinook.

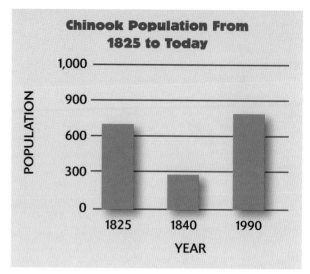

Chinook Population From 1825 to Today

POPULATION / YEAR

1,000 / 900 / 600 / 300 / 0

1825 — 1840 — 1990

This totem honors the many native tribes of Oregon that make up the Chinook Nation.

For thousands of years, the Chinook tribe lived in present-day Washington State. Their home was along the shoreline where the Columbia River flows into the Pacific Ocean. The Chinook traded heavily with other native tribes and European explorers. The Europeans first came to the region by sea. Later, they came by land. Both whites and other Indian tribes used a special language called Chinook Jargon when they traded. Until about 1900 more than one hundred thousand people throughout the West used this language to make trade easier.

European ships sailed to points along the coast of present-day Washington State to trade with the Chinook.

HISTORY

Trading with whites

In the 1500s the Chinook had their first contact with nonnative people. European explorers arrived by ship on the Pacific Coast. By the early 1800s, American and European trade ships often dropped anchor near Chinook territory to trade.

In 1805 American explorers Meriwether Lewis and William Clark became the first whites

Explorers Meriwether Lewis and William Clark were the first whites to travel by land and reach Chinook territory.

John Jacob Astor built Fort Astoria, one of the first trading posts on Chinook territory, and enjoyed a strong trade relationship with the tribe.

1929
Stock market crash begins the Great Depression

1941
Bombing at Pearl Harbor forces United States into World War II

1945
World War II ends

1950s
Reservations no longer controlled by federal government

1979
Chinook Heritage Program is begun to help establish legal status of tribe

1989–1990
The National Museum of the American Indian Act and the Native American Grave Protection and Reparations Act bring about the return of burial remains to native tribes

1993
The government agrees to review the tribe's petition for federal recognition

to reach Chinook territory by land. By that time, the fur trade had become very profitable. John Jacob Astor was the wealthy owner of the American Fur Company. In 1811 he built a trading post called Fort Astoria on Chinook land. The white people who lived at the fort were called Astorians. At first, the Chinook did not like this invasion of their territory. They soon changed their minds. The tribe began a strong trade relationship with the Astorians.

Over the next twenty years, many traders and settlers invaded the tribe's lands. The whites brought new illnesses with them. The natives had never been exposed to these illnesses. Their bodies were unable to fight off these diseases. Between 1830 and 1840, nearly two-thirds of the Chinook tribe died of an illness they called the cold sick. This illness might have been a form of flu. As the tribe struggled with this severe outbreak, their lands were taken by white settlers. In 1851 the Chinook signed the Tansey Point Treaty. This agreement was to give the tribe land and water rights in their ancestral territory. The U.S. Senate, however, did not approve the treaty.

The angry tribe refused to sign the next treaty set before them. This treaty would have forced the Chinook to share a reservation with the Quinault Indians, their old enemies. As the tribe's lands were

This drawing depicts the Quinault Reservation, where the U.S. government forced the Chinook to live with their old enemies in the late 1800s.

taken over, the Chinook ran out of choices. Most Chinook were finally forced to live with other tribes on reservations in Washington and Oregon. They became part of the Warm Springs, Yakima, Chehalis, Quinault, and Grand Ronde Reservations.

The tribe fights the government

Around 1900 the Chinook began the first of many legal battles with federal and state governments. The tribe wanted to get back money for its lost lands. The Chinook became one of the first tribes to bring a lawsuit against the United States over land claims. In 1913 the Chinook received a small settlement of twenty thousand dollars for 213,815 acres of their homeland.

Later that year the tribe fought to get pieces of land, called allotments, on the Quinault Reservation. At that time, Indian reservations were broken up into allotments. These were plots of land privately owned by Indians. As they fought for their allotments, the Chinook also helped to create the Northwest Federation of American Indians.

Shoalwater Chinook gain recognition

During the twentieth century, the Chinook won only a small sum of money from the federal government in legal settlements. This was only a little of the money

the tribe had wanted to make up for their lost land. Whites had taken almost 750,000 million acres of Chinook land. In 1932 the Chinook people were finally given allotments on the Quinault Reservation. The rest of the Chinook lived with other Native American groups or in their own homes in small towns and cities.

The U.S. government has recognized only one of the three major groups of Chinook. In 1979 it recognized the Chinook who share the Shoalwater Bay Reservation with Chehalis and Quinault people. Without federal recognition, a tribe does not exist as far as the government is concerned. The tribe cannot get government help.

In a rare victory against the U.S. government, the Chinook won rights to their ancestral fishing areas in 1974.

Efforts to gain recognition continue

The Wahkiakum Chinook have not won recognition. They live on the Quinault Reservation. The tribe had one victory in 1974. They won a case against the U.S. government that gave them the right to fish in their ancestral fishing areas. It also gave them one-half of the fish caught by Indians and non-Indians at those sites.

The third group is called the Chinook Indian Tribe. It was recognized by the state of Washington in 1955. The federal government still refuses to recognize the tribe as an American Indian nation. This is because of treaty problems that occurred in the nineteenth century. Because the tribe is not recognized, it cannot have land claims or fishing and gambling rights. The tribe is also unable to get money from the U.S. government.

In 1978 the Chinook Indian Tribe entered the Federal Acknowledgment Program to gain recognition from the U.S. government. In 1979 tribal elders began the Chinook Heritage Project. They collect historical and cultural data on the tribe. Their goal is to help restore some of the tribe's traditions. They also want to establish the Chinook's legal status as a tribe.

The members of some Chinook groups that are not recognized by the federal government have protested their lack of land and fishing rights.

Religion

The Chinook were religious. They believed in spirits that guided people through life. Some guardian spirits took the form of animals. Others came as invisible spirits that entered a human being's soul. Around age ten, a Chinook boy was sent on a vision quest to meet his guardian spirit.

The design on this rock represents a Native American spirit. The Chinook believed that objects held spiritual powers.

The Chinook also believed that all objects had powers. Christian missionaries were upset to see

CHINOOK JARGON

The Chinook language was used to form a special trade language. It was called the Chinook Jargon. The language was used by traders during the eighteenth and nineteenth centuries. It began as a mixture of languages spoken by tribes of the Northwest. These tribes had gathered to trade with the Chinook near the Columbia River. Later, when the Chinook began large-scale trading with Europeans, the Chinook Jargon added words from many other languages. Chinook Jargon even had Japanese and Russian words. Chinook Jargon was used throughout the Northwest from Alaska to California. In the early 1900s, English replaced the language.

Some examples of Chinook Jargon are *hootch*, which meant "homemade liquor"; *tzum SAM-mon* meant "spotted salmon"; P*AHT-lum man* meant "drunkard"; B*OS-ton il-LA-hee* meant "United States"; and *TUP-so KO-pa la-ta-TAY* meant "hair."

the Chinook worship statues and wooden objects. Both Catholic and Methodist missionaries eventually gave up their efforts to convert the Chinook. Around 1900 many Chinook adopted the Indian Shaker religion. This religion is based on a mix of traditional native and Christian beliefs. Its followers are called Shakers. When they experience the power of God, they shake, groan, and cry.

Government

Chiefs of Chinook villages were members of the tribe's highest social class. The position of chief was passed from father to son. Chiefs were in charge of the game that hunters and fishermen brought back to the village. They handed out food however they liked. Chiefs could also sell orphans into slavery.

In 1925 the tribe formed a business council to help gain land allotments and protect their fishing rights. Today, the Chinook Tribal Office in Chinook, Washington, is the site of the tribal government.

Economy

The Chinook were successful traders. When the tribe caught too many fish, they traded the fish to other Indian tribes. Some of these tribes lived as far away as the Rocky Mountains and Alaska. The skins of sea otter, beaver, elk, deer, and bear were used to make prized hides. First, the skins had to be scraped, stretched, and smoked. The Chinook also traded basket hats and other handmade objects. The Chinook had a strong trade in whale blubber and canoes. Both men and women were traders.

The Chinook traded with the Europeans for items such as teapots, swords, pots, pans, and buckets. They also traded for tobacco, cloth, and blankets. Chinook traders packed these goods into canoes. Then they sailed away to trade the goods with other tribes. They would sail as far as two hundred miles away. They traded their items for furs that they could trade back to the Europeans. Over time, few fur-bearing animals were left in the area because of they had been overhunted. The tribes also traded canoes, animal horns, copper, baskets, and slaves. The Chinook also traded a type of shell called dentalium. These shells were used as money.

Today, many Chinook make money by fishing in the Columbia River and the Pacific Ocean. Some make yearly trips to Alaska to fish or to work in canneries there.

The Chinook carved canoes like this one and traded them with other tribes. Chinook traders also traveled by canoe to exchange goods with Europeans.

DAILY LIFE

Families

Chinook children were given a lot of attention by their parents and grandparents. Children respected their elders for their wisdom. Once children learned to walk, their mothers no longer carried them. Boys swam whenever they could. Men fished and hunted, while women took care of the children. Chinook women also sewed, wove baskets, gathered food, and made blankets. According to the accounts of Lewis and Clark, the women were treated very badly. They were bought, traded, or won by gambling. The women were put to work by their husbands so they could buy more wives.

Buildings

The Chinook lived in large, rectangular houses. The walls were made from thick boards of cedar wood. The thatched roofs tilted at a sharp angle. The houses stood about eight feet high. Each house was twenty to sixty feet long and fourteen to twenty feet wide. Up to ten families lived in each house. A Chinook village was made up of a long row of about thirty houses.

The inside of each house had an open living area. There was a fire in the center of this room. Smaller rooms surrounded this open space. The different families slept in these small rooms. The doorway and inner walls were decorated with colorful paintings. The floor of hard-packed dirt was covered with woven mats. The beds were woven out of cedar bark or long, hollow plant stems. When they left the village to hunt or trade, the Chinook built lightweight shelters to protect themselves from rain.

Each Chinook house was big enough to house up to ten families. Separate rooms for each family surrounded a space shared by all the inhabitants.

Clothing

Because of the constant dampness, the Chinook did not wear leather. (It would have been ruined). Instead, they wore clothing made of plant material. Men wore mat robes. Their wide-brimmed hats were made of bear grass or cedar bark. Women wore knee-length, fringed dresses made of silk grass or cedar bark. In the winter, they covered themselves with fur blankets. They wore robes made from the skins of dogs, muskrats, rabbits, and mountain sheep. Women sometimes twisted strips of fur together with feathers to make winter dresses. They tattooed their skin. The Chinook wore ear and nose rings made of teeth, beads, and copper.

The Chinook used plant material to make clothing like this woven hat (left) and skirt (right).

Food

The Chinook used dugout canoes to catch fish and sea mammals near the mouth of the Columbia River. Their canoes were up to fifty feet long. In the early spring, they used long, curved blades to rake thousands of tiny fish into their boats. Later in the year, they poked the river bottom with long, sharp poles to catch sturgeon. These fish weighed hundreds of pounds. The highlight of the fishing season came in late spring. This was when the Chinook salmon made its yearly swim up the Columbia River.

When the Chinook salmon (pictured) swam upriver each spring, fishermen could catch many of the sacred fish.

   The tribe thought of the salmon as sacred. The Chinook offered part of the year's first catch of salmon to the gods during special ceremonies. They used nets and hooks to catch many fish. The meat was dried for trade or to eat later. Harpoons were used to hunt sea lions and seals. These sea mammals sunned themselves on the rocks near the mouth of the Columbia. The tribe also gathered clams and oysters. If a whale washed up onshore, they ate its meat. Bows and arrows were used to hunt deer and elk.

Chinook hunters used harpoons (pictured) to hunt seals and sea lions.

   Women gathered plants and fruits. Favorite foods were cranberries, crab apples, cow parsnips, wild celery, and skunk cabbage.

Children of the tribe learned the skills they would need from their elders.

Education

Chinook children were taught the importance of hard work. Girls helped their mothers gather food, water, and wood. They learned how to make baskets and weave mats out of plants. They also learned how to dry fish on racks or hang them from the ceiling to smoke. Boys learned how to hunt, fish, and build houses. They also learned how to make tools, build canoes, and make nets to catch fish.

Healing practices

There were two types of Chinook healers. Both were respected and sometimes feared by the people. Doctors called *keelalles* gave medical help. The *etaminuas* helped the souls of dying people travel safely to the land of the spirits. Children learned during their vision quest if they would be healers when they grew up. The chosen ones trained for about five years. Then they began to heal people on their own.

Healers often used power sticks to rid people of evil spirits. The Chinook believed that evil spirits made people sick. The power sticks were covered with grease and decorated with feathers and paint. Healers often spent many days chanting. As they chanted, they beat the sticks on special boards or on the sides of houses. Sometimes, they found an object in a patient's body, such as a piece of wood or a stone. This object was a symbol of the evil spirit. These objects were destroyed in a special ceremony.

Arts

The Chinook carved bowls and utensils from wood and animal horn. They decorated everyday items with patterns of parallel lines. These lines were curved to look like waves or teeth. Women wove baskets from plant material, such as roots, bark, or rushes. First, they twisted and bent several ropes of tree root into a shape. Then they wove in more ropes across the shape to make the sides of the basket. Designs might be animal shapes or geometric patterns.

Men and women carved or painted their family's symbol on everyday objects. These objects included sticks, dance rattles, and boards.

The Chinook used animal horn to make bowls (left) and other utensils and plant material like tree roots to weave baskets (above).

Literature

Children listened carefully when elders told stories about the ancient days of the tribe. Sometimes, the children were asked to repeat a story exactly as it was told. No mistakes were allowed. The stories of Chinook life were not written down. This repetition made certain that the stories could be told the same way over and over again.

This illustration depicts a Chinook legend. Chinook elders used storytelling to pass down the tribe's history and beliefs.

CUSTOMS

Social classes

Chinook society had three social classes: the upper class, commoners, and slaves. The small upper class included chiefs and their families, warriors, leading shamans (pronounced *SHAH-munz* or *SHAY-munz*), and traders. (Shaman is another word for "medicine man.") The largest group was made up of commoners. Although they could become wealthy in their work, they rarely were allowed to rise above the class they were born into. Sometimes an outstanding person, like a great healer, was allowed to join the upper class.

Slaves, the lowest class in Chinook society, worked canoes, gathered food, and performed much of a tribe's physical labor.

Slaves were usually women and children. They cooked, worked the canoes, gathered food, and cut wood. They sometimes helped the men to hunt and fish. Upper-class Chinook bought slaves from neighboring tribes. Other slaves were stolen in raids on the Chinook's enemies. Slaves could buy their freedom. Some slaves were enslaved for only a few years.

Because a flattened forehead was a symbol of beauty, upper-class Chinook molded their babies' heads to make them flat.

Head flattening

Upper-class Chinook flattened the heads of their children. Flattened heads were thought to be very beautiful. An infant was placed in a cradle. A padded board was tied to the baby's forehead to mold the head into a flat shape. The Chinook were skilled in this practice. Their children did not suffer any brain damage or health risks because of it.

Vision quest

At about age ten, Chinook boys set out on a vision quest. The quest was to find a guardian spirit. This spirit would help the child get through life successfully. A Chinook boy took a special stick with him. He traveled alone to a sacred place many miles from the village. He placed the stick in the ground. The boy fasted for up to five days until his guardian spirit appeared in a vision. The guardian spirit was often in animal form. The spirit told the boy what role he was expected to play as an adult member of the tribe. Sometimes, the spirit taught the child a special dance or song. This dance or song could be used to call the spirit in the future. If a boy did poorly at this task, it showed that he had not been brave when his spirit first visited him.

Every Chinook boy went on a vision quest to find his guardian spirit.

War and hunting rituals

War was not an important part of Chinook life. The people sometimes used violence when insulted or injured by another tribe. One account of a Chinook war dance tells of excited men who shouted war threats and fired their rifles in the air. The Chinook men wore red, yellow, and black paint. They danced in a circle and yelled loudly every few minutes. Those with knives swiped at the air. Battles rarely caused a large loss of life. Sometimes, tribes began to fight at an agreed-upon time. They fought only until the first person was killed. Then the conflict was declared over as quickly as it had begun.

Courtship and marriage

The families of the Chinook bride and groom gave each other gifts. Upper-class families traded beads, axes, cloth, knives, and kettles. The exchange was followed by a festive meal. Wealthy men sometimes had more than one wife. Some Chinook wanted their daughters to marry important Indian or white men so the family could benefit from their trading business.

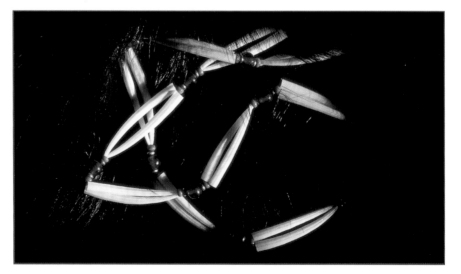

Families of the bride and groom exchanged gifts of beaded jewelry (pictured) and other valued items at the marriage ceremony.

The Chinook "buried" some of their dead, along with the tribe member's valued possessions, in special canoes like the one in this engraving.

Funerals

Both men and women had objects that were special to them. When they died, these items were buried with them. Sometimes, bodies were placed in a canoe and hung from a tree. Cremation and underground burial in wooden boxes became common after outbreaks of disease killed many Chinook.

Current tribal issues

Today, members of the Chinook Indian Tribe still work to gain recognition from the federal government. They want the benefits that would come from it. They have run into problems because the treaty signed by their people in 1851 never became legal. Another problem is that the tribe

Tribal leaders like Gary Johnson (pictured) and other modern-day Chinook still await federal recognition of the tribe.

refused to sign a later treaty. In 1993 the government agreed to review the tribe's petition for federal recognition. At the end of the twenthieth century, the Chinook still had not heard whether they would finally receive recognition.

Notable people

Chief Comcomly (d. 1835) was a powerful Chinook leader. During the early nineteenth century, he controlled trade along the Columbia River. White traders held him in high regard. In 1805 white explorers Lewis and Clark gave him a peace medal and an American flag. After Comcomly's death from the flu in

1835, a doctor named Meredith Gairdner robbed his grave. He stole Comcomly's head and sent it to England for scientific study. After more than one hundred years of protests by the Chinook, the head was returned to the Chinook. It was reburied in 1972.

This replica of the burial canoe of Chief Comcomly, who had earned the respect of many white traders and explorers, is a monument to his memory.

For more information

Lyons, Grant, *Pacific Coast Indians of North America*. New York: Julian Messner, 1983.

Porter, Frank W., III, *The Coast Salish People*. New York: Chelsea House, 1989.

Glossary

Allotment a plot of land in a reservation

Chinook Jargon a language used by traders in the 1800s and 1900s

Indian Shaker religion a mixture of Native American and Christian beliefs

Reservation land set aside for Native Americans by the government

Shaman a Native American priest who used magic to heal people and see the future

Treaty an agreement between two or more parties

Vision quest a Chinook boy's search for his guardian spirit

Index